BOYO
BALLADS

Books by Kyffin Williams

Across the Straits (1973)
A Wider Sky (1991)

BOYO BALLADS

KYFFIN WILLIAMS

EXCELLENT PRESS

First published in Great Britain 1995 by
Excellent Press, 103 Lonsdale Rd, Barnes,
London SW13 9DA

Copyright © Kyffin Williams 1995

Illustrations and text by Kyffin Williams R.A.
By permission of the National Library of Wales/
trwy ganiatâd Llyfrgell Genedlaethol Cymru

ISBN 1 85487 803 4

A copy of the British Library Cataloguing in
Publication Data for this title is available from
the British Library

Printed and bound in Italy by G. Canale & C.,
Torino

ACKNOWLEDGMENTS

These illustrated verses were noticed in the National Library by Sir Jeremy Chance as he was making a study of Welsh art, and it was he who suggested that they should be seen by the public. Consequently they were exhibited for the first time in Plas Glyn-y-weddu in 1993 where they were seen by the Marquess of Anglesey. It was he who suggested that they should be published and it was Mr Ian Skidmore, who has for many years been interpreting the peculiarities of the Welsh Nation to the general public, who contacted the publishers.

The verses were originally created for my friends in much the same manner as Edward Lear amused the children of Lord Derby. I am grateful to the National Library of Wales for allowing them to be published.

K.W.

INTRODUCTION

BY KYFFIN WILLIAMS

In the valleys of South Wales they have a very sharp wit, a sharpness that acted as some sort of shock-absorber from the imminent possibility of death in the coal mines or in other places of heavy industry. Their wit is intentional whereas we in North Wales are humorous unintentionally and fatalities in industry come usually from a long struggle against silicosis.

The song about Crawshay Bailey was created in the valleys in order to discredit the ironmaster in his attempt to win a seat at Westminster. It was unfortunate for its perpetrators that it had the opposite effect, for he was returned with a large majority.

Crawshay Bailey, who was born in 1789, was a far-seeing industrialist who realised the importance of the recently invented railway engine. Consequently he was not only able to transport coal and steel more swiftly than before but was also able to manufacture the rails in his ironworks. The Crawshay Bailey song concentrated originally on his engines and their 'four miles per hour', but inevitably verses were added making fun of his family. The simplicity of the verses made it easy for people to add more until his family assumed unnatural proportions and the name of

Crawshay Bailey became well-known far from the valleys of South Wales. The song could be heard at many social gatherings, in public houses and rugby clubs, but I first heard it sung with inebriated vigour by both officers and men of the Royal Welch Fusiliers.

A fellow officer was my old friend Somerville Travers Alexander Livingstone Learmonth. Sandy was an expatriate Scot who had married into a local South Caernarfonshire family and had become devoted to the inhabitants of that lovely part of Wales. He and his wife lived in Tan-yr-Allt, a beautiful white house under the cliffs of Tremadoc once occupied by Percy Bysshe Shelley during his unfortunate residence in Wales. He had infuriated the local farmers by shooting sheep that he believed to be suffering from scab. The farmers rebelled and Shelley fled to safer climes.

Sandy seemed to love people indiscriminately and was unfailingly courteous. As a fellow Celt, he understood the eccentricities of the Welsh and they in turn accepted him as one of them.

He was the Chairman of the Porthmadog bench and often I had breakfast at a large table presided over by his housekeeper Miss Annie Parry in the company of a sergeant of police, a warden of the National Park and a Breton onion seller.

Sandy Livingstone Learmonth had been to school at Winchester, was a great lover of English literature and had a passion for the works of Rudyard Kipling from which he could quote at length. The verses of Crawshay Bailey came to him as light relief. He enjoyed their lunacy and he contributed many to the saga.

For many years I used to stay at Tan-yr-Allt, for Sandy and I had much in common and it was an excellent base for a landscape painter. On leaving after one of my visits I invariably left a present in the form of an illustrated verse about one of the monstrous family. Over the years these became part of a large collection and when Sandy died his daughter Jean asked me to deposit them as a gift to the National Library of Wales.

To save the land from harm he
went and joined the British army
and reviewed a whole Battalion
On his fiersome coal-black stallion

Crawshay Bailey's brother Rupert
He was made the Mayor of Newport
But is now in deep disgrace
He was steal the Borough mace

Crawshay Baileys brother Mike
Had a little motor bike
He was go right round the Gower
In a quarter of an hour.

Crawshay Bailey lost his fears
Joined the Royal Welch Fusiliers
He is now a man of note
with the Fusiliers goat.

Crawshay Bailey's brother Dave
He was very strong and brave
And we all admired his skill as
he played goal for Pontardulais

Crawshay Bailey's brother Stanley
He was very tall and manley
He played Rugby, golf and hockey
and at times he was a jockey

Crawshay Bailey's sister Alice
Was the cook at Lambeth Palace
But she burnt the Bishop's haddock
So was sent home to Llangadog.

Crawshay Bailey's sister Gwen
was a smart equestrienne
She was join her brother Joe
In Bill Cody's Western show.

A hogin Rhydyclafdy.
He wass very very crafty.
He wass flog pheasants Nanhoron
In Pwllheli for a coron.

Crawshay Bailey's brother Tomos
He has now departed from us
For he went and caught pneumonia
In the mountains of Snowdonia

Crawshay Bailey's sister Anna
She was play the Grand Piana
She was also play the fiddle
Down the sides and up the middle

Crawshay Bailey's sister Bella
Had a little umberella
And she was so pleased about it
She was never go without it

Crawshay Bailey brother Billy
He played lock for Caerffili
But those forwards from Llanelli
They was trample on his belli.

Crawshay Bailey craved adventures
But he went and broke his dentures
So no longer does he roam
For he's staying now at home

Crawshay Bailey's brother Dic
Was at shootin very quick
But in tryin to shoot much quicker
Shot Aneurin Jones the vicar.

Gawshay Bailey craved for Knowledge
So he went to Cardiff College.
He didn' do much thinkin'
But an awful lot of drinkin'

Crawshay Baileys had an engine
It was puffin and a'blowing
and it had such mighty power
It was go four miles an hour

Crawshay Bailey's sister Ethel
She was go to Capel Bethel
Just to hear the dulcet tones
Of the reverend Mostyn Jones

Crawshay Baileys brother Geoff
He was sent off by the ref
For the English he was kickin 'em
On the rugby ground at Twickenham

Crawshay Bailey's brother Greg
Had a handy wooden leg
When the boys were playing cricket
They was use it for a wicket

Crawshay Bailey's sister Gwladys
Oh it very very sad is
For she's living so they say
With the boys of Tiger Bay

Crawshay Bailey lived at Rhyd
And his poor old nose did bleed
For those fellows from Blaen Nantmor
They was hit it with a hammer

Crawshay Bailey's sister Harriet
Drove a little pony chariot
And everyone did see her
Trying to be like Boadicea.

Crawshay Bailey's brother Hector
Was a sanitary inspector
He worked at Llansantffraid
That's why all the people died .

Crawshay Bailey's brother Iolo
He was dream of playing polo
And he borrowed from a croney
A wild Welsh mountain pony

Crawshay Bailey's brother Jac
Said I must go now and pack
Before it's dusk, I'll be in USK
ar Breakfast I'll be back

Crawshay Bailey's brother James
was a terror for the dames
and he chased them night and day
From the Gower to Colwyn Bay

Crawshay Baileys brother Jim
and there wasn't much of him
But was quite another thing
When they put him in the ring.

Crawshay Bailey's brother Joe
Played for Cardiff second row
But he kicked a fellow's teeth in
So is now with Cefneithin.

Crawshay Bailey's sister Mai
She was fishing on the Wye
But a salmon most gigantic
Dragged her out to the Atlantic

Crawshay Bailey's sister Maude
She was searching for the Lord
But she met a boy called Evan
and is now in seventh heaven

Crawshay Bailey's brother Moses
He was suffer from neurosis
And at times of wild euphoria
He was think he's Queen Victoria

Crawshay Baileys sister Nancy
She was very smart and fancy
And now living in the manse is
with the reverend Eli Francis

Crawshay Bailey's cousin Pugh
He did <u>not</u> know what to do
For some said that "glas" was green
While some others say its blue

Crawshay Baileys brother Rhys
He was join the local Police
and he now maintains the law
In the streets of Cwm-y-glo

Crawshay Bailey he played football
with a great detirmination
He did play the Rugby Union
Not the soft Association

Crawshay Bailey's sister Ruth
She was really most aloof
To avoid the local people
She was climb the parish steeple

Crawshay Bailey thought he'd kill
Spanish bulls down in Seville.
The occasion over-awed him
For the bull it went and gored him

With his next-door neighbour Sid Rees
He was climb up Cader Idris
It was very very frightening
With the thunder and the lightening

With his little cocker Spaniel
Fond of sport was brother Daniel
He was hide six brace of grouses
In the pockers of his trousers

Crawshay Bailey's brother Vince
and I haven't seen him since
He held up the Dowlais mail
And was sent to Cardiff gaol

Crawshay Bailey had a wife
Who was cause him pain and strife
And because she was a sloven
He was put her in the oven.

—